Presented to

With love from

As sure as seasons are made for change,

Our lifetimes are made for years.

So I will be here.

I Will Be Here

Steven Curtis & Mary Beth Chapman

J. Countryman

Nashville, Tennessee

This is my beloved,

And this is my friend.

SONG OF SOLOMON 5:16

A Note about the Song

hen my parents divorced after almost thirty years of marriage, Mary Beth and I walked through the valley of confusion and heartbreak that followed. As with many songs before and since, I wrote "I Will Be Here" as I wrestled. How would my wife and I handle the ebb and tide of emotions and feelings that would accompany life's changes? Would we still "be here" for each other—until one of us placed the other in the arms of Jesus? This song became a testament of my commitment—and recommitment—to the bride whom I had promised to love until death parted us.

I still remember the first time someone suggested that "I Will Be Here" might become a favorite wedding song. How strange it seemed to me! This song didn't immediately conjure up images of beautiful flowers, long white dresses, and soft candlelight in my mind. Instead, I pictured a man and woman standing against the wind, holding each other's hands, with a look of steely determination in their eyes. Obviously, I hoped that this song would challenge and encourage others in their own journey into the wonderful mystery called marriage, but I truly had no idea how much of an impact the song would have on so many who were beginning that journey. I feel very honored that this song has been a part of such a significant event in the lives of others. I can't think of a more appropriate message to want to communicate on that day, a message I feel even more strongly now that I am sixteen years into the journey that began for Mary Beth and I in October of 1984.

One of the reasons I am excited about this book is that it encourages couples to consider what it truly means to "be here" for one another. Mary Beth and I have even included some very personal notes and letters in hopes that our honesty and vulnerability might encourage other couples to be honest and vulnerable with each other.

STEVEN CURTIS CHAPMAN
FALL 2000

I Will Be Here

GENESIS 2:24; MATTHEW 19:5–6

Tomorrow morning if you wake up
And the sun does not appear,
I will be here.

If in the dark we lose sight of love,
Hold my hand and have no fear,
'Cause I will be here.

CHORUS

I will be here when you feel like being quiet;

When you need to speak your mind, I will listen.

And I will be here when the laughter turns to crying;

Through the winning, losing, and trying, we'll be together,

'Cause I will be here.

Tomorrow morning if you wake up

And the future is unclear,

I will be here.

As sure as seasons are made for change,

Our lifetimes are made for years,

So I will be here.

CHORUS

I will be here, and you can cry on my shoulder;

When the mirror tells us we're older, I will hold you.

And I will be here to watch you grow in beauty,

And tell you all the things you are to me;

I will be here.

I will be true to the promise I have made,

To you and to the One who gave you to me.

Our Marriage

He who finds a wife

finds a good thing,

And obtains favor

from the Lord.

PROVERBS 18:22

I have said many times that I believe the greatest gifts God has given us are our relationships. First and foremost, He gave us the gift of a right relationship with Himself through His Son Jesus Christ, which enables us to experience right relationships with each other. Only because of His faithfulness and His grace can we truly learn what it means to be committed to one another in love.

Nowhere have I come to realize more about my need for the grace and mercy of God than in my relationships with others, especially my precious wife. God has brilliantly designed us in such a way that we need and desire to be in relationship with others, and yet those very relationships will reveal our own selfishness and sinfulness and show us our desperate need for God if we will allow it.

Second, He has given us the most wondrous and mysterious of all human relationships through marriage. As I say "mysterious," I can almost see some of you nodding your heads in agreement, or maybe even scratching your heads. I am the president of the "want to have it all figured out" club, and

this "mystery" business is one part of marriage I didn't really plan for. (I don't remember seeing it in the color brochure.) The real challenge is, the longer I'm in it, the more I realize that the mystery is not just a part of marriage, but it is the essence of marriage.

I'm learning that my wife of sixteen years, whom I think I know better than anyone on this planet, is a wonderfully mysterious woman who longs to be known. So for me, the words "I will be here" mean I not only want to keep "showing up," but I also want to embrace all that my wife is and is becoming. I want to be a "student of my wife," as my pastor says.

Mary Beth and I are very uniquely different in the way we approach and think about certain things. We process information very differently, and I can foolishly allow that to drive a wedge between us instead of seeing it as an opportunity to learn more about her. In the lyrics to the song "I Will Be Here," I reaffirm my commitment to "be here" when she feels like being quiet and when she needs to speak her mind. This line in the song, like many others, is deeply personal because of the struggles that we had early on in our marriage; when things got too quiet, I would try to get Mary Beth to tell me what she was thinking. I came from a family of externalizers who talked a lot about what they felt, but Mary Beth came from a family who didn't communicate as openly. I broke her heart and drove her away many times in my attempts to get her to talk to me and as I tried to "fix" her. I also have had to learn how to listen when she needs to speak her mind. We've all heard it said that communication is the key to marriage. The only problem is I'm one of those people who loses my keys all the time. But by the grace of God, I have an earnest desire to hear not just the words she said but what's behind the words.

Like so many other young couples in the beginning of their relationship, we were amazed at how much we had in common, and we believed that was what drew us together. As time has passed however, we have seen that we are in fact very dissimilar in many ways, and these very differences are part of God's purpose in bringing us together. Her strengths are often my areas of weakness and vice versa, and we have to choose whether to embrace or resist that part of the mystery of our relationship.

I thank God that He has ordered things in such a way that until death separates us, I will still be discovering the "wife of my youth."

Mary Beth is a fearfully and wonderfully made woman created in the image of God, and my calling as her husband is to love and honor her in a way that brings glory and honor to her Maker. Unfortunately, I am a sinner who blows it often and needs the inexhaustible grace of God. If you happened by our house some days and listened at our door to the way we are speaking to each other, you would know that we both still have much to learn.

I wrote "I Will Be Here" not because I have figured it all out; I wrote it out of a deep desire to love this one who is my best friend and my wife. Thanks be to God for the merciful patience and forgiveness that my sweetheart has continued to show me in the process. I am more in love with Mary Beth now than ever before, and I feel like I'm just getting started. That's the wonder of this mystery called "marriage."

STEVEN CURTIS CHAPMAN

But above all these things

put on love, which is

the bond of perfection.

COLOSSIANS 3:14

Sweetheart,

What a memorable week we have had together here in the Berkshires! There have been some really bad moments (driving angrily through Boston LOST or no heat in the wedding) and some really great moments (Country Curtains... thrills chills + spills, Norman Rockwell Museum and Round Rockwell Woo Hoo! AAAHAH Angelic voices.

But the absolute best part of this week has been looking beside me as we tooled along in our Explorer or reaching out as we strolled through shops and taking the hand of my beautiful bride, best friend, lover, mother of our children and pardner-for-life — and knowing that when this wonderful trip is over the absolute best part is going home with me and through the rest of life with me!! Thank you from the very deepest part of my heart! I truly do love you my sweetie!

St

—Teardrops

This is a broken heart like the one in me, because we are far apart. When we are together again it will look like this.

bandaids

Every year with you has truly been a rose,
We've watched thru tears and laughter
    as the flower blooms & grows,
And while we'd both agree there've been
    some thorns along the way,
I wouldn't change a thing, I cherish
    every single day!

You are
a precous
gift from God!

I can't wait to share another day with you!

I Love You.

I Love You.

Yours for the rest of my life,

Therefore what God has

joined together,

let not man separate.

MARK 10:6–9

*T*ime is a strange thing. In some ways, October 13, 1984, seems like yesterday. In some ways, it seems like an eternity ago. Sixteen years ago, on a warm, sunny afternoon, I was the blushing bride, and Steven was the dashing groom. I was all of nineteen years old; he was a mature twenty-one. As I walked down the aisle that day with my arm wrapped tightly in my father's, I remember telling myself that this was it, this was forever, this was commitment. I didn't know how great or how hard marriage would be. I didn't know how many laughs or how many tears would be shed. I didn't know how hungry or how full we'd be. I didn't know so many things. I don't even know if this nineteen year

old was capable of thinking through the "long-term." But I did know I was making the promise of a lifetime—to take Steven as my lifetime mate, no matter what.

I remember driving our 1976 green Ford Pinto home from our wonderful one night honeymoon at the Clarion Hotel in Cincinnati, Ohio. The

Cincinnati Zoo had let us in for free because they saw that our car was decorated "just married," which was a good thing because we only had about $50 to our names. We were truly living on love! After our romantic visit to the zoo, we headed toward Nashville. We literally cried all the way because reality hit us in the face. The weight of life—and learning to live it together as man and wife—came crashing in on us. We weren't worried about everyday comforts and things like whether we would eat or not. We were still childlike enough to have the faith that God would take care of our physical needs. It was the realization that we wouldn't just HAVE a wonderful marriage, we had to MAKE a wonderful marriage.

That first year of marriage taught us many amazing things about each another, things that we seemed to overlook while caught up in the "dating game." One, we learned that whoever coined the phrase "opposites attract," was completely right. Talk about two people who were as different as night and day! He was a night person; I was a morning person. He was disorganized; I was the queen of containers. He would not go to sleep angry; I would fall asleep in the middle of his best "Don't let the sun go down on your anger" speech. Needless to say, God's sense of humor at bringing us together taunted and reminded us of that wonderful wedding day not so long ago when we promised each other to stay married for a lifetime. The honeymoon was indeed over on that tearful, fearful drive home, and it was time to put into action what we'd vowed we would do.

Many things, good and bad, have come and gone in our lives to break, shape, and mold us into the individuals we are, as well as the committed couple that we've grown to be. Whether it was our first-born daughter who arrived just sixteen short, difficult months after our wedding day, or the fire that destroyed our apartment when that same bundle of joy was just six weeks old, God began teaching me about the kind of commitment it takes to not just BE married, but to STAY married.

A lot has happened in our sixteen short (or long, depending on what kind of day it has been) years of marriage. Our marriage has blessed us, tried us, hurt us, surprised us, shaken us, and changed us—all for the better. But the one thing that it hasn't done is destroy us. It's a daily decision to live in a loving relationship with the man that God gave me for a husband. I am in it for the long haul. It isn't always fun. As a matter of fact, it's probably hard more often than it is easy. But I believe that's where God teaches us the most about ourselves and our sinful, selfish ways. In certain moments, God can do heart surgery and begin to change us from the inside.

I love, respect, and honor my husband more today than ever. It's a love that keeps growing and changing on a daily basis. Again, it is not a fairy-tale life without its hurts. At times, I feel like quitting, like walking away. But to know that the promise is being kept by both of us, and that we vowed that promise before God, is to know the end result. If God allows us to grow old together, we'll be sitting in our rocking chairs some day, laughing at all the great memories, and crying over the sad ones. There may be some "what ifs," and there may be some regrets, but one thing will remain: the promise between two people and their God to be there for each other for always.

MARY BETH CHAPMAN

Marriage is honorable

among all.

HEBREWS 13:4

I will be here when you feel like being quiet,

When you need to speak your mind, I will listen.

And I will be here when the laughter turns to crying;

Through the winning, losing, and trying, we'll be together,

Steven.   'Cause I will be here.

You captured my heart ten years ago
with a beautiful smile. You always knew
what to "do" or "say" to make "it" (what-
ever "it" happened to be) better. All these years
later, you still hold my heart prisoner.
I know that making "it" better, has become
a bigger challenge for you because I am
definitely not low-maintenance. However,
you continue to be the music in my
life that makes me dance! (and smile!)

I love
you
Beckie

pray for me. I know as I lay here sleeping that I am loved by you. I can't even begin to love you back the way I have been selflessly loved but I will take my lifetime to try.

I love you, always

Beth

🙂
xox

P.S.
Cuddle me when you get home please?

Every thought I have whether it be good or difficult has one common denominator.... you! I don't mean that in a bad way. It's to let you know that in a very good way, you have permeated every part of me. We are truly one.. I guess that's why all this junk hurts so much. I wish at times it would just get better... I NEED IT TO DESPERATELY.. but I will try to hang on to the process being what truly teaches us the lessons God has for us. As long as we have each other (Christ) we can make it (I want to believe this with all my heart). Please stay close to me. I'm really hurting right now.....

Happy V.D   I ♥ U!

Beth
xox

Our Friends &
Family

The first time that I saw Dan, he was leaning against the wall of our high school after finishing football practice. I was immediately attracted to him and asked him to dinner with my family that night. It was "love at first sight." We dated throughout high school and married in college. Eighteen months later, our first daughter was born. At this time, the fairy-tale romance met reality. There was now someone dependent upon us!

Over twenty-four years of marriage and seven children later, we continue to learn about unconditional love and true commitment. We have learned to laugh and enjoy our differences. The bond between us grows stronger with each experience. God's love is the glue that holds us together. When things are hard and I want to turn and run the other way, I remember the times we have shared and look into the faces of our children and choose to stay. God's unconditional love for me has no boundaries, and nothing I say or do will change His love for me. My desire is to love my husband that same way.

When I walked down the aisle on our wedding day, I had no idea how hard this road ahead would be. When all is said and done and I look into Dan's eyes, I know that we are committed to love one another for better or worse, for richer or poorer, and until death parts us. Our commitment is not just an agreement we have made with each other, but a lifelong promise that we made before God.

TERRI COLEY

erri and I were young when we met. Much has changed. However, there has been a constant—something unchanged, something I rarely talk about, but something important to me to tell Terri more often. It's about her place within me. The constant has been and remains the process of oneness that God methodically and mysteriously creates. His faithfulness to lead that process is the journey upon which I choose to remain. Terri, here is my attempt to tell you why I want to be here for you.

On August 7, 1976, we promised, "till death do us part." I will be here because I promised. But there is more, much more, because I fail at promises.

I will be here because of the seven who watch and follow us.

I will be here because you expose me and you stay.

I will be here because of the glory and the pain associated with surrendering to each other, giving birth to the sweet oneness for which Christ joined us.

I will be here because I'm loved as I am and not as I should be.

I will be here because my father wasn't, and as you well know, I barely survived the pain.

I will be here because my mother remarried two years later and a father, who is still here, adopted me.

I will be here because of who I am when I am with you . . . because of who I am when I am not with you . . . because of what I see when I look in your eyes . . . and because of what I see when I'm not looking at you.

TWENTY-EIGHT

I'll be here because of where we've been and because of where we are going. I promise again, "till death do us part."

Terri, I LOVE YOU and I WILL BE HERE!

DAN COLEY

Grow old along with me!
The best is yet to be,
The last of life, for which the first was made:
Our times are in His hand.

ROBERT BROWNING

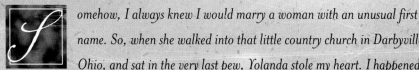

omehow, I always knew I would marry a woman with an unusual first name. So, when she walked into that little country church in Darbyville, Ohio, and sat in the very last pew, Yolanda stole my heart. I happened to be singing that night, and at the very moment our eyes met, I knew without a doubt that she would be the one I married. Three years later, at a family picnic, Yolanda's father, the Reverend Sonny Gabbart, performed our wedding ceremony.

Yolanda didn't know what she was getting herself into. Her new husband was an art teacher, a basketball coach, an artist, a songwriter, and a musician. I climbed the ladder of success, becoming the head basketball coach at a tiny Cedarville, Ohio, high school, but in 1989, I was fired. The pain Yolanda endured during the entire ordeal must have been great, but she handled it gracefully. Soon after, Yolanda also endured the stress of selling our dream home and moving to Tennessee.

In 1994, I quit my teaching job in order to pursue a career in the music industry. I left the stability of steady employment, something that is extremely important to a wife, to join a country group named 4Runner. Our group had a great run, but in 1997, our record label closed its doors. Of course, Yolanda was there, lending support to her "has been" husband whose career had ended before it even got started.

By this time, we had four wonderful children—Jordan, Canaan, Bethany, and Abigail, but I had no job, no career, and no noticeable income. Yolanda to the rescue!

Yolanda started working full-time, and I became a househusband. At one point, I signed a contract with a Christian publishing company, but after the first four books, my contract was not renewed.

As I read back over this, I ask myself, "What kind of husband would put his wife through such terrible ups and downs?" A husband with dreams . . . big dreams and a wife willing to share those dreams. We always believed that God had a reason for our travails. The only thing that mattered was that we were together, that we continued to pray for each other, and that we grew closer through our experiences.

To call her "a faithful sidekick" would be unflattering. To call her "dependable" would be an insult. She's been more than that. I'm not even so sure that the term angel would do her justice. She thinks not of herself, but thinks first of the needs of her husband, her children, and her friends. She epitomizes the song "I Will Be Here."

We recently decided to adopt a baby from China, and our roles are now reversed. How can I be there for her if I wallow in self-pity? I can't. So here we go again. Yolanda, I WILL BE HERE for you, just as you have been there for me. Please forgive me one more time.

JIM CHAPMAN III

or all twenty-eight years of our married life, my wife, Darlene, has been persistently and mercifully present in the life of a husband who needs much of God's grace. She is my love, my hero, and my model.

With the beginning of the new millennium came the breaking-in of a fresh and disruptive work of God in my self-protected heart. Darlene was very much there for me. For thirty-nine years, I had avoided going to my mom's grave. She was killed in an automobile accident when I was only eleven. So devastating was the loss that I had been running from the healing journey of grief for nearly four decades.

When it became obvious that God wasn't going to let me run any longer, it was Darlene who sat with me as I began to look at old photos of my mom and to weep the stored up tears of many years. It was she who encouraged me to drive the five hundred miles to Mom's grave.

It was Darlene who stood there with me under my arm, holding me tight and shedding her own tears, identifying with my pain and longing for my freedom. She graciously continues to invite my stubborn and unbelieving heart into more healing and repentance.

Because of her, I have a clearer picture of the face of Jesus, a better understanding of the gospel, and a fresh taste of the liberating power of God's love.

Darlene, I love you.

SCOTTY SMITH

Love...

rejoices in the truth; bears all things,

believes all things, hopes all things,

endures all things.

Love never fails.

1 CORINTHIANS 13: 4–8

'll probably always remember when Steven asked me to contribute to this book. We were walking through Frontierland at Disneyland somewhere between Big Thunder Ranch and Big Thunder Mountain and were interrupted mid-conversation by an autograph seeking church group that happened to recognize him. I contemplated, as Steven signed autographs, what I could possibly share about my marriage that would interest anyone. Steven can crank out a heartfelt love song for Mary Beth and the whole world wants to sing it, but what can I possibly offer?

In pondering this little dilemma, one thought kept coming to mind, *Blessed*. I think that is what best categorizes my marriage of thirteen years to Kari—Blessed. So via this gracious invitation to write in this book, I offer my wife a simple letter of thanks for the incredible blessing she has been to my life.

*D*ear Kari,

I could never really put into words how much I love you. The joy you bring to my life is only comparable to the joy I have in Christ, our Savior. What a blessing.

You gave me four incredible children, which you unselfishly sacrifice for daily. You manage all the things in our household so that I have a place of rest at the end of each day. You support me when I have lofty dreams, and you love and comfort me when they don't succeed. What a blessing.

You challenge me spiritually, and encourage me to serve in our local body of believers. You stood by me as my career path went through changes, and you did it without complaining. And when I was anxious, you were the first one to remind me of God's sovereignty. You constantly seek godliness. What a blessing.

You have always maintained a sense of humor and made life fun for me and the kids, from singing ridiculous made-up songs around the house to planning great vacations and special occasions. And when the kids ask me who my best friend is, I love to see the smiles of security on their little faces when I, without hesitation, answer, "Mommy is." What a blessing.

I love you,

RICK DEMPSEY

Where love is, there God is also.

LEO TOLSTOY

Love one another

fervently with

a pure heart.

1 PETER 1:22

ear Rick,

I can honestly say that if my life ended today, I would say that my greatest

joy on this earth has been being your wife. You encourage me when I am

down. You show me love when I don't deserve it. Your touch warms my heart. Your hap-

piness fills our home with love. But most of all, I appreciate your constant smile. I always

know that when you come home from work, now matter how hard your day has been, that

you are truly excited to be with me and the kids. Our children are so blessed to have you as

their daddy, and they will be the first to say it. Words cannot express the love I feel as I

think back on our thirteen years together. You have been such a wonderful example to me

as a man of God who truly desires to honor the Lord in all that you do. I am thankful for

God's sovereign plan in choosing you as my husband. Thank you for all that you have

been to me on this journey called marriage.

I love you!

KARI DEMPSEY

When I met Kent, I thought he was the kindest man I had ever met. I remember his genuine love and concern for living according to God's Word. That character would take us far in the life we were to lead together.

Kent always comes back to God's Word for his decisions and his love for me. Knowing that God's Word never changes gives me a great sense of stability in our marriage and in Kent's love for me.

One time in our life was particularly hard due to Kent's profession. The media jumped on a chance to bash Kent's faith due to some struggles in his career. They chose to call Kent "meek" (what they thought was a weakness) and pointed out that he wasn't aggressive enough to be successful. A Bible study teacher once showed me that God's definition of meek is "power under control," or even more descriptive "velvet covered steel." I realized that this described Kent beautifully, with his gentle, kind ways and his rock-solid stand for Christ. He is the leader God has provided for me—one with strength and the control of the Holy Spirit.

My husband is easily loved and respected.

PAMELA BOTTENFIELD

amela,

On October 25, 1991, I chose to make public my most sincere feelings for you. I didn't write the song because I was so eager to play the piano and sing in front of everyone (you know that scares me to death); I did it because I wanted everyone we knew to realize how deeply my affections ran for you.

I also wanted those who were closest to me to know I wasn't making a commitment to spend the rest of my life with just a pretty face, but with a woman whose beauty, wisdom, kindness, and grace fills the lives of those around her—a godly woman of commitment and compassion.

What makes the words to this song ring truer every day is that you know me so well, yet you continue to choose to hear me out when I'm unbearable, sit with me when I'm emotional, and love me when I'm unlovable.

Outside of eternal life, you are the greatest blessing God has given to me, and I will still love you unconditionally because you're worth every bit I have!

In Christ's love and mine,

KENT BOTTENFIELD

Pamela's Song

Lord, you've blessed me with a lot in life
But none so great as here today
When I will take this one to be my wife
I will love her as you say

Yes, I will love her unconditionally
'Cause she's worth every bit I have

I know this because she's yours Lord,
you've filled her with your wisdom
I thank you for the ears to hear
"Her heart is like a flowing river
Filling every heart that's near

Lord, we're standing here together
With only you inside our hearts
We know through you we'll stay together
And with you we'll never part
And yes, we'll love you unconditionally
'Cause you're worth every bit we have
We know this because we're yours

Therefore a man shall leave his father and mother and be joined to his wife, and they shall become one flesh.

GENESIS 2:24

e have been married now for thirteen years, and God is still blessing our marriage. It has been a pretty crazy time of many trials, but in the process God has "grown" us—both individually and as a couple.

The largest trial that Ray and I have had to endure is the death of our daughter. (She was our oldest, eight years old at the time, a precious little girl who loved God and loved life.) It is hard enough to understand death, but the death of a child, your own child, is even harder to understand. Erin was killed instantly, Alex was in critical condition with head trauma, and I had a fracture to my cervical spine. Ray was not with us that night. I do not remember much about the car accident itself, but what I do know is that God called Ray to walk in some very hard places, both as a husband and as a father. I remember very clearly the softness to Ray's voice, the calm look on Ray's face, the gentle tears that filled his eyes, and the tenderness to his touch. The words he spoke were very clear. When Ray told me that Erin had not survived, he had an incredible strength and love. God was very present for Ray, and in return, Ray was very present for me. Ray has always loved me, but that night and the days and months to follow, he loved me in ways that I had never felt before. Ray had realized that God had called him to surrender all things to Him, including his family. The blessedness of possessing nothing has freed Ray to love me in ways that only come from God.

It has been almost three years since Erin's death. Alex has recovered beautifully from head trauma, and since the arrival of her brother, she is loving life even more. David, our one year old, is a joy to all who know him and a blessing to our family. I have recovered from neck surgery and am adjusting well to life with an eight year old and a toddler. Ray is still the love of my life. We don't always understand each other nor do we always agree, but every day is a new day. Every trial, whether large or small, is an opportunity to love better and more completely or to push each other away. Ray and I have (most of the time) chosen to allow God to knit us closer together.

I love Ray more deeply today than ever before. I pray that God will continue to challenge me so that when I fall at His feet, I know that the love I want to give to Ray only comes from our Heavenly Father. I also pray that I will freely give that love to Ray regardless of the day or the situation and will require nothing in return.

LORI MULLICAN

There is no happier life
But in a wife;
The comforts are so sweet
When two do meet.

WILLIAM CAVENDISH

hen we first met, Lori was a beautiful, insecure twenty-two-year-old woman looking for something. God graciously put me in her path. We met and were engaged just thirty-three days later. Within six months, we were married.

At first, Lori really desired the spiritual insights that I had as a young man but sometimes resented it as well. Over the past thirteen years, Lori has grown into a godly woman who dwarfs me. I really look up to her. But her growth (and mine as well) did not come without many hard times. In the first year of marriage, we were burglarized. The third year, a tornado hit our condo (while we were in it) and left us safe but homeless for five months. In the fifth year, Lori agreed to move from Nashville to Denver so that I could go back to school. We had a new baby and no money and no job. We arrived in Denver to find that we would be living the next year in a converted ROTC camp.

Since then, we have been together through two business failures, near bankruptcy, nine job changes, not to mention my intermittent struggles with mild depression. All of these events caused stress and pain, but Lori was and still is so willing to follow me as I follow my heart to where God leads.

In January of 1998, Lori and our two daughters, Erin and Alex, were in a violent car accident that killed Erin, required Alex to be resuscitated, and threw Lori thirty feet through the window of the car, causing neck and other injuries. In the days, weeks, and years that followed, Lori has demonstrated her love and commitment to me in so many ways. She has ministered to our entire community as they embraced her. Instead of becoming bitter, she has offered hope to so many by selflessly giving herself. Alex suffered severe separation anxiety, which required Lori to spend almost a full year at school with Alex while in pain and discomfort herself. Throughout the process, Lori was patient and caring, refusing to be embarrassed by the outbursts of anger that came from Alex. She loved Alex so well, and today, Alex, without the aid of medication, is working through her loss and loving others well.

There have been many times of struggle where Lori and I have disagreed and were angry for periods of time, but God has been so good to keep us on the same page as we have moved toward Him. We are still in process of learning more each day. But one thing I have never worried about is whether or not Lori or I will be there the next day for each other. God made me a rich man the day he blessed me with Lori.

RAY MULLICAN

Many waters

cannot quench love.

SONG OF SOLOMON 7:7

When Ernie and I decided to adopt a child from Romania, we filled out reams of paperwork describing what we could and could not accept. The documents described our preference for a female child between six and eighteen months of age, with no permanent handicaps. On my fourth day in Romania, I saw Michael.

Michael was three years old and very disabled. I immediately knew that I could not live my life wondering what might happen to him. I called Ernie. From thousands of miles away, with almost no information, knowing only that this child was going to require more than we had anticipated, Ernie said simply, "Just bring him home." This could be the end of the story of Ernie's courage. However, I realize now that the real courage came after the initial commitment.

Michael came home from the orphanage with many diseases, the worst being muscular dystrophy. It is in Ernie's everyday parenting of Michael and his siblings that my husband's real character is shown. Ernie tackles everything with humor and faith. Whether teaching Eric to drive (a car or a golf ball), giving in to Maggie's requests when she calls him "Papa," reading to Carmen's first grade class, or begging dealerships for brochures of Michael's favorite car, he does it with steadfast love and joy. These things demonstrate a father's unwavering devotion to his children and family; they make a family work. For that, I am eternally grateful.

CHERYL JOHNSON

ince our wedding day on August 21, 1982, my wife Cheryl has never ceased to amaze me with her ability to "be here." Actually, that trait was visible long before our marriage. While going to college at Mercer University in Macon, Georgia, she held down a job on weekdays. Her free time on weekends was devoted to being a "big sister" to a soon-to-be teenager in town. She was there for all those questions that young people ask, and often, simply being there was all that mattered. Her selfless approach to life has never diminished; her purpose has never wavered.

Is there one incident that stands out the most in our married life? There are too many to count, but I vividly remember Thanksgiving Day of 1984, which we spent in a children's hospital with our first-born infant son. Then at two months old, Eric was having surgery to fix a digestive problem. Kids are resilient, and parents, I discovered, need each other desperately at a time like that. Cheryl was there.

In 1991, it was Cheryl who suggested that we adopt a child from Romania. It was Cheryl who traveled there while I stayed in Atlanta with Eric and our first-born daughter, Maggie. It was she who fell in love with the first child she saw there. And it was she who brought Aurel "Michael" Johnson home with the promise that she would be here for him.

The sobering reality of a doctor's pronouncement that Michael had muscular dystrophy has only intensified her vow. And she has been there for me on those days when that reality is difficult to accept.

There is not a day that goes by that I don't thank God for the blessing that is our family. From Carmen, who was eight months old when we adopted him from Paraguay in 1993; to Michael and his inspiring spirit; to the two kids, Eric and Maggie, who so quickly opened their hearts and minds to the idea of international adoption. They know what it means to "be here" for their siblings, and to witness that devotion is staggering.

I've told Cheryl before, and I repeat it here as I peck away on the computer from a Minneapolis hotel room, away on business: that woman in Atlanta, who is taking care of our kids, is a Proverbs 31 wife.

"She watches over the ways of her household,
And does not eat the bread of idleness.
Her children rise up and call her blessed;
Her husband also, and he praises her:
'Many daughters have done well,
But you excel them all'" (v. 27–29).

ERNIE JOHNSON

I love you,
Not only for what you are,
But for what I am when I am with you.
ROY CROFT

fter almost five years of marriage, Will and I are still giddy when we are together. My co-workers are amazed at how excited I am to hear his voice on the phone each time he calls.

Several qualities in our relationship fuel and sustain our love. We pray for one another numerous times each day. Prayer keeps us focused on Jesus.

We laugh often. When we can laugh at one another and ourselves, we recognize that we are not perfect. We also strive to serve one another. It is true that the more you give, the more you receive. Will is better at this than me. He constantly strives to serve me in any way that will make my day easier.

Marriage is teamwork. Will and I do the housework together, we pay the bills together, and we care for our daughter together.

Because we often go for days and weeks without seeing each other, communication is crucial for us. We have logged countless hours on the phone, and it is worth every penny.

One of the final qualities that we share is grace. When we fail each other, grace lessens the pressure of expectation and allows us to mend the hurt. When our focus leaves Christ, grace leaves the equation.

I thank the Lord each day for my precious Will and for his prayers, his laughter, his servant heart, his grace, and most importantly, his love.

JANET DENTON

T he very fact that Janet married a musician in the first place merits an entire book about the many outstanding qualities she demonstrates on a daily basis. Chapter titles could read, "Patience: How Musicians Put the 'Long' in Long-Suffering" or "Peace: The Rehearsal in the Basement is FINALLY Over."

All joking aside, I am so thankful for Janet. She fills my life with such joy and wonder that it seems impossible to me that I could love her any more than I already do.

All I have ever really wanted to do is play the drums, and I am so thankful for the opportunities God has given me. Nonetheless, leaving home to go on the road is never easy. Though we both feel my profession is a calling, it doesn't make the separation any less painful. Before we were married and still today, Janet hands me a little package of envelopes right before I step out the door. Each one is dated for a particular day and city that I'll be traveling to. Inside is usually a card, maybe a picture, or some sort of note just for me. I can't even begin to tell you how much I look forward to opening that envelope at the very end of my day. I feel like a kid waiting for Christmas morning. Reading her notes and thoughts to me gives me such a sense of togetherness, even if I'm on the other side of the country.

Thank you, sweet Janet.

WILL DENTON

My Dear Husband,

So much of who I am is you . . . your thoughts are now my thoughts, and where we differ I hope the Iron makes us sharper. You are the man of my life, and no one will ever really know the love that I have for you. I feel completely free to be my silly, controlling, serious, creative, beautiful, sporty, gutsy, hyper, sensitive, cry-baby, business woman, organizing, decorating, somewhat cooking, fingernail biting, forgiven, legalistic, dancing, wanna-be self. You are my soul mate, and when I am with you, my soul soars. You stimulate my mind, you challenge my structures, you forgive me with compassion, and you truly cherish me.

My smile is in the thought of you. How can I be a refuge for you? How can I create a home of peace and a place where we serve the Lord? You reassure me that the Lord has complete control over our lives and our questions. I am thankful for you and your pursuit of the truth. I am thankful that truth is more important to you than popularity. In my thoughts, I am praying for you constantly. You are love, and love is handsome.

FRAN KING

That their hearts may be encouraged,

being knit together in love,

and attaining to all riches

of the full assurance of understanding,

to the knowledge of the mystery of God.

COLOSSIANS 2:2

y Love,

I do not have the time to say all that I want to say. You are sleeping. The day has escaped us again, and I so want you to know the depth of my love for you. I do not say it enough. If a day or a moment were all I could have with you, I would rather have the precious moment with you than ten lifetimes without you. I find myself thinking of how I could win your love again and again, over and over.

You are my hero. There is no one else on earth I love more than you. There is no one I admire more. I esteem you. You continue to surprise me with your character and depth. If I had not met you, I would have never read or loved to read the way I do. I would not like The Sound of Music or Trip to Bountiful. You have made my life more full and rich.

Life is a journey, and the beauty and the point is not the feast, not the prize, but the hunger. It is our hunger that makes us embrace, and it is our hunger that makes us fight. I am so thankful to be walking with you.

I have written this poem for you.

What mind can measure what soul can search
the joy of a book like the one who has learned to read.
And who can celebrate the thoughts they contain

or the leather that binds truth unbound by its reading
like the man who has learned how to learn.

What man can taste the sweet nectar of peace
drink it deeply, and know the cost of his quenching
like the soldier who has done battle and lived to tell the tale.

What journal can detail the journey what novel can depict the drama
what sonnet can describe the passion like the blind man made to see,
the deaf man made to hear, the leper made to feel
or the dead man come to life

No book could I ever read No battle could I fight
No taste could I taste No picture could I paint
No place could I go No sight could I see
No beauty could I know No thing could teach me more
than loving you and you loving me.

WES KING

ike and I sat down to lunch with a young woman whom he had been counseling. Before her husband left her, he said, "If we really loved each other, we wouldn't have to work so hard to make it last." I then thought back to a seminar I attended as a young wife. The speaker wanted to know what one word we would use to describe our marriage. An older woman quickly spoke up and said, "Work!"

Marriage is work, a work in progress, but hopefully it is the kind of work that, most days, one wakes up excited to do. It would be easy to say we are still together because we love each other, but even staying in love is work. Why we are still together goes back to the beginning. We married for love. We knew God had called us together and so we made a vow before God and man to keep ourselves only for each other. It was a vow that said, "God, you've called us together. You alone know what is ahead of us, but with you it can be done!" It is in working together with the Lord, in hardships and in pleasure, that makes our marriage last.

Knowing that God is in this marriage with us means that it is something worth working for and worth holding on to. Marriage is about loving God and loving one's spouse. It means thinking more of the other person than yourself. Marriage is also about not trying to make your spouse meet needs that can only be filled by God. Once these priorities are in order—God, spouse, self—marriage becomes a work in progress, blessed by God.

RINDA SMITH

*a*s we spent time together early in our relationship, I saw God give me a love and concern for her. I wanted to meet her needs, even at the expense of my own. I knew this desire did not come from within me. It came from God. This gave me confidence to ask her to be my wife. I did not have confidence in my ability to be her husband, but I knew that if God was in this marriage with us, we could move forward with hope and anticipation.

Ecclesiastes 4:12 says that a cord of three strands is not easily broken. Our marriage is a marriage of three cords, the two of us and the Lord! Rinda and I have tried to create an environment where oneness can flourish. We do not make oneness happen. We can plant and water, but God causes the growth. Oneness comes from learning to cherish one another, spending time together, praying together, playing together, working together, and struggling together. You see that togetherness and valuing one another is key to creating the environment of oneness. When I see Rinda as a part of myself, it helps me move toward her and cherish her as I do my own body. She is part of me now.

I am able to love Rinda because I have been loved by God. As I receive His love, I am able to extend it to her. Staying close to and dependent upon the Lord becomes vital in enabling me to love Rinda well. God has called us together, so if we are both submissive to the Lord, it will take God to separate us!

MIKE SMITH

ere I am, ten years after the ceremony, and the one thing that holds me to this marriage can be explained as simply as "his eyes," or as complex as the circuitry of the computer I am using to type these words. From those weekly counseling appointments in my first year of marriage, I remember only one thing vividly. The gifted therapist was puzzled by my choice to shut down such a well-established single life and move across the country with my husband. The therapist asked me, "Tell me, what it is you love about him?"

No one—from the jaded to the most sentimental—could have predicted what would happen in me. Tough and career minded, I was intact! Yet to my shock, I folded over like a woman in labor and sobbed, saying in broken audible bits, "It is his eyes . . . they are kind." If he had asked me the color, I wouldn't have been sure. But I knew the content.

Now after ten years, after changes in him and changes in me that make us seem like entirely different people, I can still say that despite doubt, hurt, and trembling at the invitation to intimacy, there remains the truth of what was in his eyes when we dated. I am still the newlywed looking into those eyes of calm and goodness. The best gift the counselor could have given me was the question. I stated all that I needed to know and all that would be sufficient when the pain of commitment would burn hotter than the promises I made before the witnesses to my vows. Yes, pain did scorch at times, but nothing took away my soul answer—my truest inward truth about the man that I married.

Today folks recognize the importance of looking at one another in a marriage. Specialists in relationships are saying that a sustained look into the eyes of a loved one everyday can be the key to the ongoing exchange of love and trust. When someone mentioned it to me, I thought, Of course!

I know that even on the occasions when my husband's eyes have became clouded with rage or fear that I have had a place in bringing them back to safety or strength for us. And God has done His part to build in us a fledgling belief that we would rather hear hard truths and be brought back to life than have our eyes go grey—muted and opaque with distance. God is looking out for the quality of Al's inner sight. Together we fight for his eyes. Just as he and God fight for the loveliness in the eyes.

Truly the eyes are the window to the soul. And in this crazy marriage of mine, they are a thermometer and a compass. You could never have told me I would grow in beauty. You could never have told me that my husband would grow in strength and even more kindness in his eyes. Resisting looking away has born its fruit. Staying here to be looked at has been awfully, terribly naked. . . . and awfully, terribly good.

NITA ANDREWS

*T*en years ago, in the presence of family and friends, I looked into Nita's eyes and spoke our marriage vows. In essence I said, "I will be here." On that day, I committed to be there for my wife, no matter what occurred. When I spoke those words, I believed them, and I meant them. When I met her, I felt like Adam must have felt when he met Eve—"Bone of my bones, flesh of my flesh!" She was the woman I'd prayed and longed for.

I now realize, a decade after I spoke my vows, that I had no earthly idea what I'd committed to on that romantic and holy day. As I look back at the man who uttered those words, I recall of the words of C. S. Lewis in the poem "As the Ruin Falls," "I speak of love. Even a parrot can talk greek." Though I meant every word I said, I don't believe I understood them, or at best, I spoke them naively. For if there's a hurt that my wife has endured above any other, it has been my lack of presence. In short, there have been times that I've left.

There hasn't been a physical lack of presence, but rather an emotional one. Sometimes as I've gotten angry or disappointed, I've pulled away emotionally from her, withdrawing to a safe place where I can stew or pout. Other times, I've put on a veneer of pretense that looked like kindness, but in reality, was the not-so-distant echo of anger. And when I've LEFT her in those ways, she hurts, feeling the loneliness and ache that comes with the void created by my absence.

If there's something that I desire in the years to come, it is that we'll continue to strive to SHOW UP in our marriage. I want to be here, to be present both in the joy and passion of a relationship with my wife, and the times of struggle as well. I want to enhance her loveliness with presence rather than mar it with withdrawal. That's what I committed to. That's what I want to live.

AL ANDREWS

*M*y husband, Tracy, has always been there for me. God brought us together, and I cherish the love we have because it is so sweet and true.

I have a precious memory of a time when Tracy responded to God's urging and was there for me. It was shortly after our fourth child was born, on a school morning in winter. Tracy was out of town, and I had been struggling with postpartum blues and exhaustion.

On this morning, I was trying to be really upbeat, patient, and positive. I started my day in prayer, but by 9 a.m., I was in shambles emotionally. Our ten year old was in a panic that he had lost his report card, our baby had been awake every hour throughout the night and was now very fussy, and our five year old had a pre-kindergarten project due. During this chaos, I banged my head on a cabinet, and I was now dizzy and on the verge of tears. As if that were not enough, I stood, staring blankly, as our twelve year old cried out, "I just tore my last pair of contact lenses!"

My shoulders and countenance drooped a little more with each occurrence. I felt defeated and discouraged. Satan had succeeded in destroying my forced optimism.

At the peak of my despair, the phone rang. It was Tracy. I heard his voice, and I crumbled. He was tender, understanding, and encouraging. He knew just what I needed. He listened and told me how much he loved me and appreciated me.

Feeling better, I went on a serious search for the missing report card and instead found a letter from my husband, given to me on my thirtieth birthday. A full five pages long, it was entitled, *"100 Reasons Why I Love You."* I sat on our bed and read every word. It started:

Dear Becky,

Happy Birthday, wonderful lady. I've put lots of love and thought with this birthday letter, and I want you to know that I mean everything I say. Here is a list of 100 reasons why I love you.

1. I love you because you have a loving heart. . . .

100. I love you because I could never love anyone else.

I read the last line and laid back on our bed, holding the letter to my heart, and I looked up to God, smiling and laughing through tears. I thanked God for using Tracy's heartfelt, loving words to rescue me again.

I am thankful God gave me a more precious husband than I could ever imagine. He is my best friend, and I love him more than I can say. He constantly makes me laugh and smile, and I know that he will always be there—on good days and bad.

BECKY HENRY

*S*ometimes in life, it hits you right between the eyes. You are just blown away by the total overwhelming feeling of "this is meant to be."

The first time I met her, something was incredibly different. She had the most beautiful smile I had ever seen. Our first conversation lasted six hours, on the porch steps of a college building. All my plans for the day were immediately cancelled within the first fifteen minutes of that conversation. My life had instantly taken a new direction. Although I didn't know it at the time, I had found the life-long partner my God had planned for me.

Some twenty-one years later, I consider myself extremely blessed. I would also like to say it has been error-free, but it has contained many tears and a few sleepless nights. I do believe the trials, which could have destroyed us, have indeed strengthened us. Her commitment to God and family is truly remarkable. Our four children are realizing more each day what a wonderful person God has also blessed them with.

She means more to me each passing year. I am trusting in our Lord that this is a natural progression that will never end. She is my greatest friend in the world, and I selfishly pray for extra years to spend with her. I could not imagine a more wonderful heart to grow old with.

Thank you, Father.
TRACY HENRY

I am my beloved's,

And my beloved is mine.

SONG OF SOLOMON 6:3

Beth,

I need you. You're my toughest critic + my biggest fan! I'll see you soon!

Love
SL